THE BEST NEWS YOU WILL EVER HEAR

THOMAS JAY OORD AND ROBERT LUHN

russell
media

Boise, Idaho

Published in Boise, Idaho by Russell Media

Web: http://www.russell-media.com

This book may be purchased in bulk for educational, business, ministry, or promotional use.

Tax-deductible donations are accepted for the distribution of The Best News You Will Ever Hear.

For information please email customerservice@russell-media.com

ISBN (print):   978-0-9829300-5-2
ISBN (e-book):   978-0-9829300-6-9

Cover design and layout by Drew Steffen.

Printed in the United States of America.

Library of Congress Cataloging-in-Publication Data

Oord, Thomas Jay and Luhn, Robert.
   The best news you will ever hear /Thomas Jay Oord and Robert Luhn
         p. cm.
Includes bibliographical references.

ISBN (print):   978-0-9829300-5-2
ISBN (e-book):   978-0-9829300-6-9

Library of Congress Control Number: 2011921806

CONTENTS

PREFACE

The title of this book is true.

You are holding a book that tells the best news you will ever hear. Ever! We are not exaggerating.

Not only is this news the best, your life will change when you hear it. By the time you finish reading, you will be a new – and better – person. We guarantee it.

If you receive this news, you will steadily become a better person in the days, weeks, and years ahead. The news will take you on an excellent journey. The news is that good!

So… prepare yourself. Open your heart and mind. Focus your attention and read carefully. Get ready to be different.

This news should change your life – for good – forever!

1
GOD IS NOT
MAD AT YOU

A FATHER'S LOVE

A father had two sons he loved deeply. One day, the younger son said, "Father, give me today my share of the wealth I am to inherit." The father granted this request and divided the wealth between his two sons.

The younger son took his inheritance and left for a distant country. He squandered it there in wild living. He wasted his money on selfish desires, prostitutes, and foolish risks.

After the money was gone, a severe famine came to that country. Without funds for food, the young man became hungry.

In desperation, he asked a citizen of that country for work. He took a humbling and difficult job feeding pigs. While working, the young man longed to fill his own stomach with what he gave the pigs. But he had nothing.

One day, the starving son admitted his life was miserable. He said to himself, "My father's hired men have food to spare. But I am living among pigs and starving to death! I will leave this place and return to my father. I will say,

'Father, I have sinned against heaven and against you. I am no longer worthy to be called your son. Would you take me as a hired man?'"

The young man left the distant land and returned home.

While he was still a long way from home, the young man's father saw him. Compassion filled the father's heart. He ran to his wayward son, threw his arms around him, and kissed him.

As they embraced, the son said, "Father, I have sinned against heaven and against you. I am no longer worthy to be called your son."

But the father said to his helpers, "Move quickly and bring the best robe and put it on my son. Put a ring on his finger and sandals on his feet. Bring the fattened calf and cook it. We are going to have a feast and celebrate! For my young son was once dead and is now alive! My son was lost, but now he is found!"

The helpers did what the Father instructed. A celebration began.

At this time, the older son was in the fields. When he approached home, he heard music and dancing. The older son asked a helper, "What is going on?"

"Your younger brother has returned," the helper replied. "Your father is cooking the fattened calf to celebrate, because your brother is home."

The older brother had been working hard. He grew angry when he heard this news. He refused to return home to celebrate.

When the father heard his oldest son would not return, he went out into the field to plead with him.

But the son said, "It's not fair! All these years I have been working hard, and I have never disobeyed. Yet you never gave me even a young goat so I could celebrate with my friends. Now when this son of yours, who has squandered his inheritance on prostitutes, comes home, you cook the fattened calf. You celebrate for him but not for me!"

> "We are going to have a feast and celebrate! For my young son was once dead and is now alive! My son was lost, but now he is found!"

"My dear son," the father replied, "I love you too, and you are always with me. Everything that remains is yours. But because your brother was dead and now is alive, and because he was lost and now is found, we had to celebrate and be glad!" (Luke 15:11-32)

WHAT THIS STORY MEANS

Almost two thousand years ago, Jesus of Nazareth told this story. He told it to describe God's love. This story is good news. The good news is this: God loves you, us, and everyone!

Sometimes we live like the younger son in the story. We waste our gifts, talents, and resources on wild living. We live a life of selfishness and unhealthy pleasure.

As a result, we feel like we are feeding pigs. We feel as though we are starving to death. The life of wild living leads to destruction and death.

Sometimes we live like the older son in the story. We are angry that others get more than they deserve. We think we deserve more. We work hard believing we must earn approval. We never disobey, but we fail to enjoy love.

Working to earn love leads to bitterness. It sucks the joy out of life.

> God loves us.
> God forgives us
> and calls us to
> return home.

Whether we are selfish or bitter, the good news is God loves us. God forgives and calls us home. God offers us a joyful life!

Like the father in the story, God embraces us with open arms. When we return from wild living or the bitterness of trying to earn love, God and others celebrate! God comes out to meet us, because God loves us extravagantly.

THIS BOOK IS FOR *YOU*

We wrote this book to tell you the best news you will ever hear: God loves you and is calling you home! In fact, God loves everyone and is working to establish the reign of love everywhere.

God has always loved you. God's love is deeper than the deepest ocean and wider than the universe. It never fails. God constantly seeks to save the lost.

God's love is steadfast, enduring, and everlasting. God is faithful to us and loyal to all creation. His love never fails. We can count on God to love ALWAYS (Psalm 36).

As the authors of this book, we believe God is calling you home. Why? There are many reasons.

One reason is we have heard God's loving call in our own lives. We are responding by returning home and living in the joy of God's family.

Another reason we think God is calls you home is that we believe the Bible tells us this. In fact, we are convinced. The story above and others in the Bible describe God's deep love for you and all creation.

As you read this book, you will discover that we draw from the Bible to talk about the good news of God's love.

The Bible is a very old collection of writings that God inspired in a special way. It will be our primary resource for understanding God's love for us and why we should love others as ourselves.

There is a third reason we think God is calling you home. We believe God quietly stirs within our hearts a desire to return to love. While you read this book, you will feel that stirring.

We are sure God is already "talking" to you. God's way of communicating is usually a small, inaudible voice. A "stirring" is like an intuition or sixth sense. Some call it a strong feeling.

The Bible was written thousands of years ago. God uses the Bible to offer healing. The Bible's main purpose is to tell us God loves us and we should love.

In your heart of hearts, we think you have probably already heard God saying, "Come home and live in my love."

We encourage you to say "yes" to God's invitation.

BIBLE EXPLANATION

You will often see names and numbers in parentheses at the end of sentences in this book. They will look something like this: (Luke 15:11-32).

The names refer to the "books" in the Bible. These books have poetry, letters, teachings, historical accounts, songs, and more. The Bible is a massive collection of writings.

The numbers indicate particular chapters and verses in the Bible. Long ago, scholars divided the books into small segments. These small segments have numbers to help us locate verses.

We encourage you to read the Bible on your own. But you do not need to read the whole Bible to understand its core message. The goal of this book is to give a concise presentation of the good news found in the Bible.

GOD LOVES YOU AND ME

We already said God's love is deeper than the deepest sea and wider than the universe. The Bible tells us that God is love (1 John 4:8, 16).

Sometimes in life, we need to know God loves us individually.

> God loves each of us personally. God loves me. God loves you.

To put it personally, God loves you in particular! God cares about you and wants you to live a life of meaning and joy. In fact, Jesus said that he offers us an excellent life (John 10:10).

Jesus talks about how much God loves you. He told two stories to illustrate. One story is about a shepherd and a lost sheep.

A loving shepherd lost one of his 100 sheep. He did not rest content with the ninety-nine safely in his care. Instead, this good shepherd searched for the missing one.

When the shepherd found the lost sheep, says Jesus, "he joyfully put it on his shoulders and went home. Then he called his friends and neighbors together and said, 'Rejoice with me; I have found my lost sheep.'"

Jesus also said that God is like a woman who loses one of her ten coins. After discovering her loss, she did not say to herself, "No problem. I still have nine coins. I do not care about the missing one." Instead, she found a light and searched her home carefully.

When the woman found the lost coin, says Jesus, "she called her friends and neighbors together and said, 'Rejoice with me.

GOD IS NOT MAD AT YOU

I have found my lost coin.'"

Like a shepherd searching for the lost sheep or a woman searching for her lost coin, God searches for each of us. God never gives up – ever!

God rejoices whenever any of us come home (Luke 15:3-10). We can be assured that God loves us personally.

God loves you!

GOD LOVES EVERYONE

Sometimes we need to realize God loves others, too. It does not matter one's tribe, intelligence, past history, family, sexual behaviors, looks, wealth or poverty – God loves us all!

God cares for all creatures, great and small. The love of God extends to every bit of creation!

A wise man came to Jesus one evening. He wanted to learn about the reign of love Jesus was preaching and living. "If you want to live in that love," Jesus said to him, "you must be born again."

This confused the man. How could a person be born a second time, he wondered? How could a mature person return to a mother's womb?

Jesus must have seen his puzzled look. Jesus explained what he meant. Being born a second time involves spiritual rebirth. The good news is that everyone can be spiritually born again.

> God loves the whole world. God cares for you, me, and all creation. God's love extends to everything in the universe!

"God loved the world so much that he gave his only son," Jesus told the man. Whoever believes in the son will not die spiritually. That person can enjoy abundant life (John 3:1-16).

The writers of the Bible report that Jesus is the son whom God gave. When we follow Jesus, we enjoy the abundant life of love God gives. The good life involves following Jesus' example by living a life of love.

Notice that Jesus says, "God loved the world so much…" God loves everyone. Not just you. Not just us. Not just a few. Everyone!

We are all God's favorite children.

In fact, Jesus said God is not interested in condemning anyone (John 3:17). God does not want anyone to die spiritually. God seeks to save us all.

God is not mad at us!

GOD IS NOT MAD AT YOU

God hates it when we hurt others and ourselves. Doing such things is called committing "sin," and we will talk more this later. God hates sin and wants to save us from destructive behavior. God hates it when we hurt ourselves and others, because -- above all -- God loves everyone.

> When we were acting like enemies, God reached out. In love, God invites us to be reunited.

To enjoy the born-again life, we must return to God. We can live the good life when we follow Jesus' example. Believing in Jesus involves living in the light and avoiding deeds of darkness (John 3:18-21).

In a letter to Jesus' followers in Rome, a man named Paul talks about God's love. He says that when we were acting like God's enemies, God reached out to us. God did not act like our enemy. Instead, God invited all of us to be reunited

When we accept the invitation to be reunited, we can live an excellent life. Jesus makes this possible (Romans 5:10-11).

Like the younger son living in a distant land or the older son working in the fields, we all have lived in wrong relationship with God. But God wants a right relationship. God wants to reunite with you. It is time to embrace your loving Father.

We do not need to be afraid of God. God loves us! God loves others. And God loves all creation.

This is wonderful news!

2
GOD IS
A GOOD CREATOR

GOD CREATES A GOOD UNIVERSE

"In the beginning, God created the earth, stars, and galaxies" (Genesis 1:1). This is the first sentence of the Bible. Without going into details, it tells us God is our Creator.

After hovering over the waters and formless materials, God created all things. God repeatedly says all things are created "good." The heavens, light, earth, skies, animals, seas, plants, and people are all created very good (Genesis 1:31).

In the creating process, God asks creatures to "bring forth" others. Those whom God creates are to "be fruitful" and "multiply." God calls creatures created good to join in creating more good creation. It is an amazing project!

> God saw all that he had made, and it was very good.

The book of Genesis places special emphasis upon God creating humans. The first two chapters report that God makes male and females for nurturing companionship with one another. They are created in God's image. Although we do not know completely what it means to be created in God's image, it is clear that God asks humans to take a special role in caring for the rest of creation.

After this original work of creation, God rested for a day. We should consider this day of rest holy. Resting occasionally is something God asks us to do too. We need to take a break periodically. Too much work is not good.

THE BEAUTY OF CREATION

If we look around our world today, we see God's creative activity. One song in the Bible puts it like this: "The heavens declare the glory of God, the skies show God's handiwork" (Psalm 19:1).

God's creation is majestic, and it reflects a majestic and helpful Creator.

The beauty and complexity of creation evoke awe. Many people erupt in worship and praise. Another Bible song-writer puts it this way:

When I consider your galaxies,
the work of your fingers,
the moon and the stars,
which you have set in place,

I am amazed that you focus your
        attention on tiny humans!
        I am amazed that you care
        for our children!

You made humans a little lower than the heavenly
        beings and crowned them with glory and
        honor.

You put humans in charge of caring for all you
        made.

You put creation under their loving supervision:
        all flocks and herds,
        and the beasts of the field,
        the birds of the air,
        and the fish of the sea,
        all that swim the paths of the seas.

O LORD, our Lord, how majestic is your name
        in all the earth! (Psalms 8:3-9)

God – who made all creation – is our source of help in time
of trouble. Our good Creator works to overcome the trouble
we see in the world and in our lives.

Another song in the Bible celebrates God as creator and
our helper:

I lift up my eyes to the hills
>   where does my help come from?

My help comes from the Lord,
>   the Maker of heaven and earth.
>   (Psalm 121:1-2)

The one who created and continues to create all things wants to help in our time of trouble. It is amazing!

CREATION POINTS TO GOD AS LOVING CREATOR

Creation reveals God's invisible qualities, including God's eternal power and loving nature.

One of the most important early Jesus followers, a man named Paul, says creation points to God. Creation gives us clues about the nature of God who created all things.

"Since the creation of the world," Paul says, "God's invisible qualities—God's eternal power and divine nature—have been clearly seen. Creation reveals these invisible qualities. Because of this, humans know at least some things about God" (Romans 1:19-20).

Creation proclaims that God exists!

Perhaps the most important news that creation tells is: God loves us. An early follower of Jesus named James says God is both Creator and the Source of all good:

"Every good and beneficial gift is from above," says James. "These gifts come to us from the Father of the heavenly lights. God's love does not change like shifting shadows. God gave us a second birth through the word of truth. We are like the first fruit of all God created" (James 1:17-18).

It may not surprise us that God loves those who do good. But Jesus says God also loves those who do evil. God loves those who want to be friends and those who consider themselves God's enemies. Divine love does good to **all** others – friends or foes.

When Jesus instructs his listeners to love, he uses an example from the natural world. "God causes his sun to rise on the evil and the good," says Jesus, "and sends rain on the righteous and the unrighteous" (Matthew 5:45). God does good to everyone!

God is still in the business of creating and still in the business of doing good. Another songwriter expresses this in his prayer. He says, "When you send your Spirit, they are created. You renew the face of the earth" (Psalms 104:30). Every living creature, from humans to dogs to ants and more, depends upon God's creative and sustaining presence.

Creating continues in a special way for those who say "yes" to God. We saw in the last chapter that Jesus said those who say "yes" to God are born a second time. They experience new birth.

God can make us what Paul calls "new creations." For such people, "the old has gone and the new has come," says Paul. God has made a right relationship possible for us as new creatures (2 Corinthians 5:17-18).

God continues to create – to recreate us and to create all things – and God calls creation "good."

CREATION AND SCIENCE

Some statements in the Bible may seem strange today. They do not sound like what we would find in science books. When scientists write articles and books, they usually do not talk about God as Creator. Scientists who believe God is Creator usually do not say so when expressing the results of their research. Scientists and the writers of the Bible usually do not write in the same way.

The Bible tells us how to find abundant life. It does not tell us scientific details about how life became abundant.

Some people think they have to choose between what the Bible says about creation and what science says about the universe.

They think they must either believe God created the world and continues to create. Or they must believe what scientists call the big bang origin of our universe and the evolution of life.

We think we can believe both. We can believe the Bible's words about creation. And we can affirm the best work of science.

The Bible gives a true and faithful witness to God as the Creator. The Bible talks about **who** created – God (with creatures joining in). And the Bible tells us **what** was created – all things. It gives us clues as to why we exist and why there is so much beauty and love in the world.

But we also think science can give a true and faithful witness. Science gives us a natural account of how things come to be and how they exist. It gives us part of the answer to the "why" question, but it alone cannot give us the full answer.

Science does not usually talk about God. But it can help us live more safely and effectively. And science can give us information about the world God created and continues to create.

We might sum up the differences between the Bible and science like this: The Bible tells us how to live abundant life. It does not tell us scientific details about how life became abundant.

The Bible also tells us how to go to heaven. It does not provide the science to tell us how the heavens go.

Science and the Bible are not enemies. We consider them partners for helping us discover truth about who God is and what God's good creation is like. Theology and science can be friends.

Together, science and the Bible help us sing these words with the Psalmist:

> "The heavens declare the glory of God, the skies show God's handiwork! O Lord, our Lord, how majestic is your name in all the earth!"

3
SOMETHING HAS GONE WRONG

God always and extravagantly loves you, us, others, and all creation. God created all things good long ago and continues to create today.

So...

Why are there so many problems?

Why does pain, suffering, death, and evil occur? Why do we get sick, become confused, or hurt others and ourselves? Why are we victims of hurricanes, drought, tornados, floods, volcanic eruptions, and unexpected extreme temperatures?

And why do we do bad things? Why do we lie, cheat, and steal? Why do we murder, rape, and torture? Why do we hate, gossip, and become addicted?

If a good God created a good world with good creatures, why are things sometimes bad ?

THE FIRST ANSWER

Since the beginning of recorded history, humans have wondered why life has problems. The Bible provides several answers.

The first answer comes near the beginning of the Bible. The book of Genesis says God created a good world, and it offers a story to answer why we have so many problems. The story is about two humans named Adam and Eve.

God created Adam and Eve and asked them to care for the earth, plants, and animals. But God warned them not to eat fruit from one of the trees. Eating this fruit, said God, results in spiritual death.

One day, a serpent talked with Eve about the forbidden fruit. "You will not die if you eat this fruit," said the serpent. "In fact, eating this fruit will make you like God." The serpent tempted Eve to ignore God's warning.

Eve believed this lie and ate the fruit. She gave some fruit to Adam, and he ate it also.

Almost as soon as they had eaten, Adam and Eve felt regret. They were ashamed of their disobedience, and they tried to hide. They were afraid God would be angry.

God asked Adam, "Have you eaten from the tree? Why did you eat when I warned you not to do so?"

Adam did not want the blame for disobeying. "It is not really my fault," he said. "You gave me, Eve, my partner. She gave me fruit from the tree."

Eve quickly defended herself, "The serpent lied and tricked me." She also did not want the blame for disobeying.

Hearing this, God became sad. God knew negative consequences come from disobedience. Spiritual death comes to those who choose to do other than the loving best God asks. God said, "Because you have done this, I know you will be under a curse" (Genesis 2).

Throughout history, those who disobey God experience the curse that disobedience brings. Disobedience is a central reason we have problems today. We should not blame God for bad things caused by those who disobey the God who wants what is good.

> Spiritual death comes to those who choose to do other than the loving best God asks.

OUR BIGGEST PROBLEMS COME FROM FAILING TO LOVE

God calls us to live lives of love. When we choose to live otherwise, we, others, and creation suffer.

Paul uses a farming analogy to talk about the consequences of our choices. "You reap what you sow," he says. If you plant improper living, you reap spiritual death. But if you plant godly living, you reap abundant life.

Paul counsels his readers: "Let us not grow weary in doing what is right. We will reap good things at harvest time. Do not give up." Whenever we have an opportunity, he says, "let us work for the good of all" (Galatians 6:7-10).

Jesus told a story about the negative consequences that come to those who do bad. He said obedient and disobedient people could be divided in two groups, like a shepherd divides sheep from goats.

In Jesus' story, the sheep are blessed. They live a good life, because they help others. They feed the hungry, give drink to the thirsty, welcome strangers, clothe the naked, care for the sick, and visit prisoners. Those who act in these ways demonstrate God's loving reign in their lives.

The goats, however, live cursed lives. They disobey and choose not do good. They do not help members of God's family, those outside God's family, or other creatures. They do not demonstrate God's loving reign.

Jesus concludes his story by saying the sheep enjoy eternal life. But the goats suffer (Matt. 25:31-46).

Jesus identifies with us. He identifies so strongly with everyone that he considers what we do to each other as also done to him. Because of this, doing good to others is doing good to Jesus. Failing to do good to others is failing to do good to Jesus.

Our biggest problems come from failing to love as God asks. When we do what God advises, we gain the joy that comes from living an excellent life. If we do not love, everyone suffers.

Adam and Eve are not the only people who have disobeyed God. We have all acted like goats. We all have sown our seeds – our lives – improperly.

"Sin" is the word that best describes disobeying God's call to love. The Bible examines the problems we find in life. So it talks a lot about sin.

In his letter to Jesus' followers, Paul says, "everyone has sinned and falls short of God's glory" (Romans 3:23). To sin is to fail to do the loving best God asks.

To put it plainly: to sin is to fail to love as God wants us to love. This is disobedience.

The consequences of sin are destructive. Sin always leads to spiritual death and sometimes to physical death (Romans 6:23). Sin makes our lives and the world worse than it would have been had we responded rightly to God's call to love.

> To sin is to fail to love as God wants us to love.

The most profound sadness and harm we experience often

come from our own sin. Our spiritual death is our own doing. Sin destroys.

GOOD PEOPLE SOMETIMES HAVE PROBLEMS

Not all our problems come from our own disobedience. Sometimes others create problems and cause us pain and sadness. At the time of Jesus' birth, for instance, a jealous king named Herod tried to kill him. Herod feared Jesus would grow up to take his throne. He ordered soldiers to kill little boys in Bethlehem, where Jesus was born.

Many boys died at the hands of these soldiers. None deserved death. Neither they nor their families were reaping the consequences of their own bad choices. Yet they suffered and died.

This story and others remind us that what we do – good or bad – influences others. We are interrelated. We sometimes suffer because of someone else's bad choices. Our pain is not always our own doing.

Sometimes our problems come from nonhuman sources, like extreme weather, animals, disease, and volcanic eruptions. Natural evil occurs on our planet. Droughts and famine come. Diseases kill thousands, even millions. Innocent babies die.

The writers of Genesis attribute some problems to the negative effects of Adam and Eve's sin. Their disobedience even affected the soil God created. Although still capable of producing fruit, the soil became cursed and produced weeds to choke other plants. Our sins not only negatively affect other people, they negatively affect creation.

Sometimes our pain and suffering come from accidental events or random mutations. Jesus said some problems come from malfunctions in the created order.

Jesus once met a man blind from birth. His followers assumed someone's bad choices were to blame. They asked Jesus, "Whose sin caused this blindness? Was it the man's or his parents' sin?"

Jesus replied, "Neither this man nor his parents sinned" (John 9:1-3). This blindness was no one's fault and served no grand purpose. Jesus also talks about other natural evils

> Some problems just happen. God did not plan them for a purpose.

that are not anyone's fault (see, for instance, Luke 13:4). Sometimes bad things just happen. Creation does not always function correctly.

Paul describes the problem by saying good creation has been "subjected to frustration." Creation longs for the day when it "will be liberated from its bondage to decay" (Romans 8:20-21).

In the meantime, some problems just happen. They make no sense from anyone's perspective. God did not plan them for a purpose.

WE HAVE SPIRITUAL ENEMIES

The Bible also tells us we have an enemy who "prowls around like a roaring lion looking for someone to devour" (I Peter 5:8). Biblical writers call this enemy a variety of names: Satan, tempter, accuser, liar, evil one, and the Devil. The Bible talks about "fallen angels" who carry out evil schemes.

Satan tempted Jesus to disobey God. We are also tempted in this way. The Bible says Satan, not God, is the source of these temptations. God is good and does not tempt us to do evil (James 1:13).

Biblical writers attribute many evils to this enemy. For instance, Luke reports that Satan crippled a woman for eighteen years (Luke 13:16). Jesus encountered people whom Satan influenced so much they seemed "possessed" or owned by evil (Matthew 7:6; 9:32).

The followers of Jesus battled the demonic realm. Paul experienced torment, and he called it a messenger of Satan (II Cor. 12:7). When he tried to visit one church, he said the enemy stopped him (I Thess. 2:8).

Biblical writers talk about this evil dimension in various

ways. Jesus and his followers faced temptation and torment from evil ones. But Jesus never fell to temptation. And we never face temptation that we – with God's help – cannot bear (1 Cor. 10:13)

We have real enemies and evil systems that tempt us to disobey God. They try to persuade us to abandon a life of love. Evil ones are sometimes the source of pain, sickness, and suffering.

GOD SQUEEZES SOMETHING GOOD FROM BAD

Why would a good creation – which a good God created – be susceptible to all of these problems?

Part of the answer comes from the free choices creatures and evil ones make. Problems occur when creatures choose wrongly. But part of the answer is also that sometimes good comes from pain and suffering.

Sometimes we need harsh weather to kill viruses, for instance. Sometimes volcanic eruptions are needed to replenish the soil with nutrients. Sometimes we need rain or snow to replenish water supplies.

God inspired the writers of the Bible to remind us that sometimes good can come from suffering.

Paul says, "We know that suffering produces patience, and patience produces character, and character gives us hope.

And our hope will not disappoint us. It is based on the love God has given us" (Romans 5:3-5).

We should not think, however, that **all** pain and suffering were meant to make us or our world better. Some suffering is pointless. God does not want genuine evils to occur. God wants what is good, true, and beautiful, not what is evil, false, and nasty.

Not all natural disasters are ultimately good. And not all choices do more good than harm. Our loving God is not the source of the genuine evils that hurricanes, drought, disease, and eruptions cause. God does not need evil so goodness can increase (Romans 6:1).

Unfortunately, some people say God causes or allows all of these problems. They think God sends or allows evil to test us. Some people say God creates problems for some greater good. We do not need to agree with this view.

Instead of saying God causes or allows evil, we believe God works to squeeze some good out of problems God did not want in the first place. God redeems.

> God works to squeeze some good out of problems God did not want in the first place.

God works to bring good from the problems creatures cause. But this does not mean God planned these problems from the beginning. It does not mean God causes them in the present. Instead, God takes what has been broken and uses it for good.

Paul talks about this when he says, "God works for good in the midst of everything that happens. God invites those who love him to join this work to bring about good. This is part of God's purpose for our lives" (Romans 6:28).

No matter how bad things get, God is with us. God feels our pain and suffering. God works for good in the midst of bad. And God calls us to join in this rescuing work. But God should not be blamed for evil.

WHEN WE ARE THE PROBLEM

To this point, we have seen that sometimes our sin or the sins of others are the source of our problems. Sometimes evil ones cause problems. Sometimes we experience pain and suffering because of destructive natural events.

We also have emphasized that God is love. God is not the source of our problems. God does not cause evil. Our loving God wants to help in the midst of pain and suffering.

These points are important. But we need to add one more dimension to our discussion. Perhaps we might best introduce this dimension by asking a few questions:

Have you ever done something that hurt another person?

Have you said something unkind? Have you failed to love when you know you should have loved?

If you are honest, you answered "yes" to at least one of these questions.

Do you find yourself asking, "Why do I act like that? Why is it hard to love people consistently? Why am I not good all the time?"

Behind our words, actions, and attitudes lies something deeper. The Bible describes this something deeper with several phrases. Sometimes it is called a "sinful nature." Other times this deeper problem is called "the flesh" or "sin living in me."

We are not just people who sin occasionally or fail to love from time to time. We have actually become sinners. Sin so controls our lives it has become our identity: sinful is who we are. Sin becomes a habit.

> We have actually become sinners. Sin becomes our habit.

On one hand, we are made in God's image, and God deems us good. On the other hand, we all have sinned, and disobeying God has become a habit. Even though we were created good, sin so dominates that we became people who do bad things.

Paul describes this dimension of our problems with a testimony:

> I feel controlled by my sinful habits. Maybe this is the best way to put it: I am a slave to sin!

> The things I do not want to do, I end up doing. The good I want to do, I do not do. I hate it!

> The powerful habits of sin rule me. I do not feel like I am myself!

> I really *do* want to live the life of love. But I feel hostage to the habits of improper pleasure and selfishness. In my mind, I know God's law of love is right. But the habits of sin hold me captive.

> I am dying here! Who can help me out of this mess? (Romans 7:13-25)

Paul's testimony is a testimony we all have given. We have problems. We all have problems.

The problems that ruin our lives almost always originate in ourselves. Sometimes we are the problem.

Who can help us?

4
GOD'S LOVING LEADERSHIP

The best news you will ever hear is that God loves you and all creation. God loves you despite your problems, addictions, sinful habits, bad choices, and destructive behavior. God created you and everything else. And God loves you, us, everyone, and every creature!

Because God loves us all, God works to overcome problems. Overcoming problems is part of what love does. God empowers us to cooperate with this work.

THE CENTER OF THE GOOD NEWS

Jesus of Nazareth is the heart of the good news of God's love and the center of how our problems can be overcome. Many call him "Jesus Christ." Those deciding to follow him often call themselves "Christians" or "Jesus followers." The labels are not as important as God's love and our responses to God's call to love.

We earlier explored stories Jesus told to explain God's love. What Jesus said and did are also central for understanding the best news we will ever hear. In Jesus, we best understand God.

Jesus was clear about his purpose: "I came so that you can live an excellent life." Following him is the way to a right relationship with God and the way to deal with our personal problems and the problems of our world (John 10:10; 14:6).

Jesus Christ is the focal point of God's loving work. He is God's chosen one, and many call him "the Messiah." He expressed love consistently in his life, words, death, and – perhaps most surprising – his resurrection from the dead.

Jesus is the center of the good news of God's love.

JESUS IS THE WAY TO EXCELLENT LIFE

It would take many books to tell the full story of Jesus. But we offer highlights here. These should be enough to explain why we decided to follow Jesus. We tell these stories to encourage you to be a Jesus follower too.

Since the beginning of history, God has been present and expressing love to everyone, all the time. But many people remained confused. They lived in darkness. Many did not understand the depth, extent, and nature of God's love.

> Jesus came so we can live an excellent life. Following him is the way to deal with our problems.

Then Jesus entered history.

Jesus' coming was like a light emerging in darkness. He was born in a humble place – Bethlehem – and initially few people knew of his coming. Today, many people know. We celebrate the Christmas holiday in remembrance of his humble birth.

History provides little information about Jesus' childhood and early life. But in the years that followed his thirtieth birthday, he provided the best representation of God that humans have ever witnessed.

Jesus loved everyone. He healed the sick and helped the poor. He did amazing miracles to help those in need. He fed the hungry and loved his enemies. Jesus freed people imprisoned by their sinful habits, released them from the grip of evil, or healed them from sin (Luke 4:14-44).

Jesus was a savior.

Jesus loved so consistently and did such amazing things that his followers believed he was both human and divine. He said things to encourage this belief. For instance, Jesus said, "I and the Father are one" (John 10:30). He also said, "If you have seen me, you have seen the Father" (John 14:9). By "Father," he meant God.

Followers saw the connection between Jesus, God, and the life of love. Paul, for instance, advises us to "imitate God, as those who are loved, and live lives of love, in the way Jesus loved" (Ephesians 5:1).

When we imitate God, we love like Jesus. When we imitate Jesus, we love like God.

Jesus invited others to follow him. In fact, when he began his public life of loving service, Jesus said to his listeners, "follow me" (Mark 1:17). People have been following Jesus ever since.

Jesus provides the best example of how we should live.

JESUS ANNOUNCES GOD'S LOVING LEADERSHIP

The message Jesus delivered focused on God's loving leadership. He called this leadership, "the kingdom of God."

Jesus' first recorded words of public ministry sum up his message: "The kingdom of God is at hand; change your way of life and believe this good news!" (Mark 1:15) Those who believed found their lives transformed. God's loving leadership became a reality.

> Jesus loved everyone. He was a savior. He reveals what God is like.

Jesus told his listeners to make God's loving leadership their top priority (Matthew 6:10, 33). The kingdom of God is more desirable than any other thing.

God's loving leadership is like a treasure in a field for which someone sells everything to buy the field to get the treasure. It is like a beautiful and expensive pearl for which a person sells all to buy (Matthew 13:44-46). Allowing God's loving leadership to guide our lives is worth giving up everything.

Jesus said God's loving leadership is like a little mustard seed growing into a huge plant. It becomes fruitful in unexpected ways. It does more good than what we could imagine (Ephesians 3:20).

God's love changes lives, heals, liberates, and empowers us to turn from sin and evil. We are not the same when we follow God's loving leadership. We are transformed.

Jesus instructed us to cooperate with God's loving leadership wherever we find it. It sometimes emerges in the most unlikely places. God's loving leadership ought to be the focus of our individual lives, our communities, and societies.

We should not exclude any part of ourselves from God's loving leadership.

JESUS HEALS US FROM SIN

An angel told Jesus' mother the purpose of his life: "He will save the people from their sins" (Matthew 1:21). Saving people from sin is part of what it means to heal and provide an opportunity for excellent life.

Some criticized Jesus for being a friend to sinners. He ate

with sinful people, walked with them, and spent time in their homes. He cared more about being helpful than having a good reputation. He entered the messiest and bleakest situations to help people with problems.

On one occasion, Jesus' critics brought him a woman for judgment. The woman was found having sex with someone to whom she was not married. Instead of condemning her, Jesus had compassion. He forgave her and said, "Go and sin no more."

Another man named Zacchaeus robbed people by charging extra taxes. Almost everyone hated him. But Jesus chose to be his friend. He ate dinner with Zacchaeus. Because of this friendship, Zacchaeus changed. He began a new life of generosity and repayment.

Jesus not only saved from sin those he met long ago, he continues to save us today. He calls everyone to leave sinful ways and enjoy the excellent life that comes from living in love. He heals from sin those who ask.

At the end of his life, Jesus' enemies nailed him to a cross. He was punished for no good reason. A true criminal was hanging next to Jesus. That criminal asked Jesus to forgive him, in the name of God, and Jesus did immediately.

God forgives today. God will forgive your sins and ours. God forgives even the worst things we have ever done.

God always forgives those who ask.

Nothing is too bad for God to forgive.

> Nothing we have done is too big or too bad for God to forgive.

We find asking God to forgive brings us a sense of peace that surpasses complete understanding. When we say, "God, I'm sorry for what I've done," or "I'm sorry for causing so many problems," a heavy burden lifts from our shoulders. We feel release.

The best word we know to describe this feeling is "joy." We feel joyful!

God not only forgives. God makes it possible for us to live a very different life – a good life! We can be healed from the destruction of sins we committed. God also begins healing the pain others inflict.

Paul put it like this: "God rescued us from the power of darkness and transferred us into the loving leadership of his beloved Son. In Jesus we have renewed life, and our sins are forgiven" (Colossians 1:13-14).

God calls and empowers us to live a life free from the chains of sin!

GOD SUFFERS WITH US AND TRANSFORMS OUR LIVES

We not only benefit from Jesus' life, we also benefit from

his death. And we benefit from the good news that God raised Jesus from the dead (Romans 5:8).

This news is shocking. But it's true. Even death cannot stop God's love!

Despite loving everyone all the time, Jesus was betrayed. One of his followers – Judas – betrayed him and assisted those who wanted him dead. After an absurd trial, Jesus was sentenced to death.

Jesus was killed like a common criminal of his day: soldiers nailed him to a wooden cross. He suffered and died. It was tragic.

Jesus was dead nearly three days. He lay lifeless in a cold tomb. But God raised him from the dead.

Jesus was resurrected!

God validated Jesus' life and words of love by giving him life again. Jesus was vindicated in the face of critics and enemies. God gave him the divine stamp of approval!

Jesus' followers consider his death and resurrection important. His death reminds us that, in an important sense, we must also die. Jesus' followers must go through a spiritual death to their sinful ways so God can resurrect them to live life to the fullest. Jesus' resurrection gives us hope that love

– not death or evil – has the last word.

Christians use various descriptions for how Jesus' death benefits us. Some say he gave his life as a ransom for us (Matthew 20:28). Others say Jesus took our sins upon himself so that we can be right with God (2 Corinthians 5:21). His death reconciled creation to its Creator (Ephesians 2:16).

> Jesus' resurrection gives us hope that love will have the last word.

These descriptions and others proclaim the general truth that Jesus died "for our sake" (Romans 5:8). We benefit. A follower of Jesus named John the Baptist put it this way: Jesus "takes away the sin of the world" (John 1:29).

Jesus' suffering on the cross reveals that God feels pain and cares deeply. In Jesus, God experiences the kind of suffering we experience. God is the fellow-sufferer who understands our problems and pain. God empathizes with us.

Paul talks about God suffering with us and providing comfort. He says that God is "the Father of mercies and all consolation. God consoles us in all our affliction." And because God consoles us, "we are able to console those in affliction with the consolation with which God consoles us" (2 Cor. 1:3-4). God also overcomes suffering. The resurrection of Jesus gives us hope that our own problems and the problems of life in general can be overcome. Overcoming begins now and continues after we die.

God has already overcome some problems. Others will be conquered in the future.

Jesus' followers remember his death and resurrection today by eating bread and drinking from a cup. Jesus ate this simple meal with his followers just before he died. He said the bread and drink were his broken body and shed blood. He asked followers to remember him when they met together.

Christians celebrate today by eating this same meal. They call it "eucharist," "communion," or "the Lord's supper." This shared dinner becomes a powerful event for God to overcome some of our problems. And God uses it to empower us to work in response to God to make our lives and the world better.

We not only benefit from Jesus' past death, we also benefit from God's presence with us here and now. And he promised he would never leave us nor reject us! (Hebrews 13:5)

JESUS INVITES US TO RESPOND TO GOD

From the beginning of his public ministry, Jesus called listeners to respond to his message of love. Today, God calls you.

You must choose to follow Jesus. You must choose to live a life of love.

What Jesus said long ago applies to you: "Ask and you will receive. Seek and you will find. Knock and the door will be opened" (Matthew 7:7).

God gives good gifts to those who ask (Matthew 7:11). These gifts involve living an excellent life. As we seek God's loving leadership, we receive these good gifts.

> We are not the same when we allow God's loving leadership to reign.

We – the authors of the book you are reading – have asked for that excellent life. We have received it! We have decided to follow Jesus. We asked forgiveness for our sins, and we enjoy living lives transformed from bad to good. God's loving leadership brings us joy!

God invites us to cooperate with God's work to transform our lives and the world. We play a role in God's work to overcome our problems. We must ask for and accept God's loving leadership.

When we say "Yes" to God's invitation, our lives have genuine meaning and real purpose. Saying "Yes" does not mean we instantly discover answers to every question or have all our problems solved. But living in God's loving leadership provides a way to make sense of life. It gives life meaning. The excellent life God provides helps us stop acting destructively. We can live for the common good, not our own selfish desires. This is life in community, enjoying mutual affection, and expressing brotherly and sisterly love. To the extent that harmony depends on us, we can live in harmony with others.

THE EXCELLENT LIFE CONTINUES AFTER WE DIE

Like most people, followers of Jesus believe we continue existing after our hearts stop beating. In some way or another, we continue to have personal experiences after our bodies die.

The good news is that God not only guides us to live an excellent life now, God also offers a good life after our bodies die! Our personal experiences after death can be even more excellent than what is possible in our current life. The word most used to describe this afterlife is "heaven."

We can be confident those who respond to God's call to love enjoy excellent life now and later. Those who choose sin will suffer, because sin has negative consequences.

Earlier we read Jesus' words that "God loved the world so much that he gave his only son." Whoever believes in the son will not die spiritually. That person can enjoy an excellent life (John 3:1-16).

This excellent life entails a high quality of living now. But we can continue to enjoy a good life in the afterlife. God cares deeply about the here and now. But God also makes possible an excellent life after our bodies stop working.

We have seen that choosing sin causes huge problems. Choosing other than love causes destruction. It results in spiritual death.

The same is true in the afterlife. Choosing other than love causes "wailing and gnashing of teeth" (Matthew 25:29-30). The life of disobedience to God's loving leadership leads to a bleak existence – both now and later. Christians often call this miserable experience "hell."

Our hope for a good life here and now is God's loving leadership. Our hope for a better society and planet is God's loving leadership. And our hope for a good life after our bodies die – heaven – is God's loving leadership.

Jesus tells us that God's love is our hope – here, now, and in the future!

5
WHAT SHOULD WE DO WITH THIS GOOD NEWS?

There is no better news than the news in this book.

Were someone to announce that vast wealth would be yours, that news would not compare to the good news of God's love. Were you told of future fame, power, or pleasures, such news would pale in comparison to God's love. Even life itself is not as important as love.

Nothing compares to knowing God loves you and to loving God and others as yourself!

RECEIVE THE GOOD NEWS

So what should you do in response to this good news?

Receive it! Accept it! Act on it!

Let the good news of God's love orient your life. Let it become your first, foremost, and all-encompassing truth. Let God's loving leadership be the center.

> Receive the good news of God's love. Let it orient your whole life!

Most people pray to begin accepting God's loving leadership. Some ask God to forgive them. Some seek God's healing. Some people express their fears, frustration, and confusion. Some let go of problems and ask God for help.

Just about any prayer is appropriate. Words are not as important as the desire to accept God's love and live in it. God knows our deepest thoughts even when words are not fully adequate. God accepts everyone.

You may want to put down this book and pray. In fact, we encourage you to do so. It may be the most important thing you will ever do.

Right now, accept God's love and commit yourself to living a life of love. Here is a prayer that might help you if you want to receive God's love and become a follower of Jesus:

> *"God, I am grateful that you love me. I admit I have problems. I have sinned against you. I have wronged others and hurt myself. Please forgive me. I accept Jesus as my savior. I choose to follow you in a life of love. Amen."*

LIVING A LIFE OF LOVE

The Bible often calls accepting and receiving God's love "believing." Two of Jesus' followers, Paul and Silas, put it this way: "Believe in the Lord Jesus Christ and you shall be saved" (Acts 16:31). If you prayed the prayer above or one of your own, you are now a believer.

To "believe" is to do more than affirm ideas about Jesus. It means committing your life to receiving God's love and living like Jesus. "Believing" involves accepting God's loving leadership both now and throughout life.

> Accept God's leadership. Believe in the Lord Jesus Christ and you will be saved!

Often in this book, we said love is the heart of the good news. Love is the central theme of the Bible and Jesus' central message. In fact, Jesus said two commands sum up our basic instructions for life:

1. Love God with everything that you are.
2. Love your neighbors in the way you love yourself (Mark 12:28-34).

When we do these things, we cooperate with God in bringing about the salvation God intends for everyone. We enjoy the meaningful life that following Jesus makes possible. We participate in the work God is doing in our world.

Following Jesus means imitating him. Jesus loved God, and he loved others as himself. Jesus loved friends and those who considered themselves his enemies. He loved family members and strangers. He lived a life of hospitality.

God empowers us to love like Jesus. Without God's power, we cannot love. But with God, love is possible.

Embrace a life of love.

LIVING THE GOOD NEWS TOGETHER

Living a life of love is not something we do alone. Following Jesus is something we do alongside others.

Although Christians are one in Christ, they sometimes think and act in different ways. Christians should find or establish local communities that teach and practice God's love as revealed in Jesus.

Those who follow Jesus are part of a worldwide family of believers called "the church." Followers of Jesus meet in groups to seek and promote the good life to which God calls. God wants us to live in loving community with others who follow Jesus.

In the Bible book of John, we find a prayer Jesus prays for his followers. He says:

Father, you give the good life to
all who know you and me. I have made
your name known to the world. As you have sent me into the world, so I send them.

I ask that they become one, so the world may believe you sent me. And I ask that you make them one, so the world will know you love them even as you love me.

I have made known your character and heart of love -- and I will continue to make them known -- so the love with which you love me may be in them (John 17).

Jesus cares about his followers. He wants them to thrive in community as the church. In John's book, Jesus teaches his followers these things:

I am the vine, you are the branches. Those who live in me and I in them bear much fruit. Apart from me, you can do nothing.

As the Father has loved me, so I love you. Live in my love. If you keep my commands, you will live in my love, just as I have kept my Father's commandments and live in his love.

This is my command: love one another as I have loved you (John 15).

The majority of the Bible was written by and for Jesus' followers. As the church, Christians come together to follow the life-giving command to live in God's love.

A number of activities help Jesus' followers grow in God's love. You have already done one: you prayed.

Christians pray alone and together. They study the Bible and learn from other helpful resources. They frequently receive the bread and juice of the body and blood of Jesus. They sing praises and worship. Christians share their joys and sorrows, talk about temptations and spiritual victories, and encourage one another. They help one another and those not yet in the church.

When we respond to God's empowering love, we find God healing the world, our communities, and our lives. When we meet together, we and the world become better.

In the church, the power of love grows exponentially!

GOD'S LOVING SPIRIT ACTIVE TODAY

God's love has always been active in the world. When the community of Jesus' followers emerged, God revealed love in even more powerful ways. God, who is an invisible and universal spirit, empowers them.

Christians call God's empowering activity "the work of the Holy Spirit."

Jesus told his followers they could do greater things than he had done (John 14: 12-13). This is possible because God as the Holy Spirit empowers the church. Whenever those who follow Jesus' way of love gather together, the Spirit is present in a special way.

One special event occurred when Jesus' followers first met together in Jerusalem after Jesus had departed his earthly body. The Bible book of Acts reports this event.

The followers of Jesus were meeting together. Suddenly, a sound like the rush of a violent wind filled the entire house where they were sitting. The Holy Spirit filled them all, and they began to speak in other languages.

This dramatic event puzzled the people of Jerusalem. They heard Jesus' followers speaking in various languages. They wondered if they had been drinking too much wine.

One of those present – Peter – explained what was happening. "God is pouring out the Spirit on everyone who will receive!" he said.

> God's gift of the Holy Spirit brought together Jesus' followers to form the church.

After describing some of the ways people might act when God's loving Spirit empowers them, Peter said, "Everyone who calls on the name of the Lord shall be saved."

This was not the end of his Peter's speech. He also explained God's action in history and especially in Jesus.

> Peter concluded, "Change your hearts and lives.
> Be baptized in the name of Jesus Christ so your
> sins may be forgiven. Receive the gift of the Holy
> Spirit. This promise of new life is for you, your
> children, and for all who are far away – in fact, it is
> for everyone whom God calls" (Acts, chapter 2).

God's gift of his own Spirit brought together Jesus' followers as the church. They devoted themselves to learning together, eating together, prayer, sharing things in common, and giving to the poor. Amazing things – signs and wonders – occurred as the people responded to God's empowering love!

Amazing things continue to happen today when we respond to God's empowering and inspiring love. People are set free from addictions. Some are healed now, while others await full healing after they die. God removes the guilt of sin. God restores broken relationships and mends wounded hearts. Many feel the joy that comes from living life abundant.

God does miracles as we respond to the Holy Spirit!

THE GIFTS AND
FRUIT OF THE SPIRIT

God as Holy Spirit is active in all creation. The Spirit calls us – no matter our race, gender, looks, or intellect – to do good. But there is even more good news: God gives abilities, talents, and capacities. Paul talks often about these gifts. He says we should use them to promote the common good.

When talking about the gifts from the Holy Spirit, Paul makes a comparison. He says we each have one body. But our bodies have different parts, each with different functions.

Similarly, there is one worldwide community of people who follow Jesus Christ. That community is the body of Christ. Each person has been given different talents, abilities, and capacities. Each person plays a part in the body. The one body functions best when each member uses his or her unique gifts.

> Each person has been given different talents, abilities, and capacities. The one body is most effective when each member uses his or her unique gifts for the common good.

Some people are good at warning others of potential problems. Other people serve extraordinarily well. Some are gifted teachers, and others excel in encouragement. Some people have special talents in generosity. Others are natural leaders. Some people are models of cheerful kindness. There are many different kinds of gifts.

People are different, and their gifts differ.

No matter what the gifts, all people should "hate what is evil," says Paul. They should "cling to what is good." The gifts of the Spirit help us "be devoted to one another in love" (Romans 12:3-10).

The Bible provides other lists of gifts. These reveal that God's Spirit guides us to work for the common good.

For instance, some people are given the gift of wisdom. To others, the Spirit gives great knowledge or faith. Some have special gifts for healing and miracles. Some people are gifted at discerning good and evil. Others speak in unknown languages, and others interpret them.

"All these are the work of one and the same Spirit," says Paul. God distributes these gifts (1 Corinthians 12:7-11).

Not only does the Spirit give gifts to those who follow Jesus. The lives of those who respond well to the Spirit's activity show the positive results of love. These results are the fruit – the effects – of the Spirit.

The Spirit inspires us to love, gives us joy, and urges us to promote good life. The Spirit helps us be patient, kind, and generous. These are all fruit of the Spirit.

One of the most important things the Spirit does is help us control ourselves. We must have self-control so that we do not orient our lives toward gratifying our own desires.

Unfortunately, some people do not respond well to the Spirit's leading. They disobey. They seek to gratify their own desires.

Paul lists problems that arise when people reject God's loving leadership. For instance, they sometimes have sex with those to whom they are not married; they act impurely; they waste good resources; they idolize created things. Others seek power in witchcraft, start fights, wars, and quarrels. Some unnecessarily divide themselves from others. Still others get drunk and celebrate irresponsibly or waste their time on stupid activities.

Those doing these things are not living under God's leadership! Such actions lead to spiritual and eternal death.

Paul says we who follow Jesus must live according to God's loving Spirit. We must let the Spirit guide us to follow Jesus and not our sinful desires (Galatians 5:13-25).

SHARING THE GOOD NEWS WITH OTHERS

You should share the good news you have read in this book. News like this should not be kept secret!

There are many ways to share this good news. In fact, there are not enough books in the universe to describe God's love and how we can share it.

The Bible lists several ways we share the good news of God's love. Some lists describe leadership roles and activities. Others offer guidelines for living. These guidelines help us discern what love requires (Luke 6:1-11; Romans 13:8-10).

> There are many ways to share the good news of God's love.

We want to conclude this book with two general ways you might share the good news of God's love.

One way involves helping those with problems. Jesus was asked what it means to love our neighbors. He told this story in response:

> A man was going from Jerusalem to Jericho. On his way, he was robbed. Thieves stripped him of his clothes and beat him. They left him half-dead.
>
> A religious leader happened to be going down the same road. When he saw the man half dead, he passed by on the other side.
>
> A law-abiding citizen also came down the road. He saw the half-dead man and also passed by on the other side.

WHAT SHOULD WE DO?

But a stranger came where the man was.
When the stranger saw the robbed and
beaten victim, he had compassion. He went
to him and bandaged his wounds. He put
him on a donkey, took him to an inn, and
took care of him.

The next day, the stranger gave some money to the innkeeper. 'Look after him,' the
stranger said, 'and when I return, I will repay
you for any extra expense.'

After telling this story, Jesus asked his listeners, "Which
of these men do you think loved the man who fell into the
hands of robbers?"

The listener answered, "The one who had compassion on
the beaten man."

To this correct response, Jesus said, "Go and follow his example."

This story tells us that one of the best ways to share the
good news of God's love is to help those with problems.
Sharing the good news can mean acting in generous and
compassionate ways.

In fact, Jesus said we should do to others the loving things
we want done to us (Luke 6:31). Sometimes that means

loving strangers and enemies (Matthew 5:38-48). Sometimes it involves loving family and friends. Sometimes it includes forgiving those who have wronged us (Matthew 18:21-22). It often means helping those with problems.

The second general way to share the good news involves speaking or communicating with language in some way. This way of sharing involves telling others what you have learned.

At the conclusion of his book in the Bible, a follower of Jesus named Matthew tells of Jesus' final meeting with his followers. Jesus' last words were these:

> "All authority in heaven and on earth has been given to me. Therefore, go and help others in all nations learn to love."

> "Encourage them to follow me. Baptize them in the name of the Father, Son, and Holy Spirit. Teach them to obey everything I have commanded."

> Sometimes sharing the good news involves telling stories of God's love.

"And remember, I will always be with you – to the very end of the age"
(Matthew 28:18-20).

Sometimes sharing the good news involves telling stories of God's love. Those stories witness to God's ability to help us. They remind us that God is always with us and leads us to a good life, if we follow God's leadership.

Sometimes sharing the good news involves teaching and other times encouragement. Or it means carefully explaining God's love in helpful ways.

There are many ways to share the best news ever. This news is too good to keep silent!

SO...WHAT HAPPENS NOW?

If you haven't done so already, we invite you to accept God's loving leadership now.

Actually, we think God is really the source of this invitation. We are simply following God's loving leadership by writing this book for you. It is really God who invites you to accept his loving leadership and begin a life of love.

If you have done that, you should be excited! The Bible says all heaven is excited when people accept this good news!

The most important next step for you is to find others who follow Jesus. As soon as possible, find a church community. Others help you live the Christian life. Do this quickly, because you need help and you have a part to play in the body of Christ.

WELCOME TO GOD'S FAMILY!

If you have a Bible, study it with others. This can help you learn how best to respond to God's
loving leadership. You will never understand everything in the Bible, of course. But you can learn more about God's love and what God desires.

Christians do many things to respond positively to God's love. They give generously. They worship together often. Christians help the poor and those with problems. They take the bread and cup to celebrate Jesus death and resurrection. They share the good news with others.

Christians also often pray. We encourage you to do that often. Tell God your problems and joys. Ask God for guidance. Seek courage. And when you pray, listen for the Holy Spirit's nudging to lead you to live a good life.

Living in God's love means your life will change. But it is a change for good and a change for love. And that's the best news you will ever hear!

Welcome to God's family!

ABOUT THE AUTHORS

THOMAS JAY OORD is a professor of theology, ordained minister, and author of many books. He teaches at Northwest Nazarene University in Nampa, Idaho, USA.

ROBERT LUHN is an ordained minister and pastor of the Church of the Nazarene in Othello, Washington, USA.

CONTACT

For help, more information, or to find a Christian community near you, contact…

ORDERING INFO

THE BEST NEWS
YOU WILL EVER HEAR

is a book that we want to get into the hands of as many people as possible.

It is ideal for churches to give away to first time visitors, on Easter Sunday, at baptism services, and taking on mission trips.

Get it for friends and family.

We have special bulk order pricing. To purchase additional copies for friends or your church or if you are interested in making a tax-deductible donation for the distribution of *The Best News You Will Ever Hear*, please contact us at customerservice@russell-media.com.

To see other Russell Media products please go to http://russell-media.com/.